THE
AMISTAD

Essential Events

The
AMISTAD

BY ROBERT GRAYSON

Content Consultant
Richard Bell
Assistant Professor, Department of History
University of Maryland

ABDO
Publishing Company

CREDITS

Published by ABDO Publishing Company, 8000 West 78th Street, Edina, Minnesota 55439. Copyright © 2011 by Abdo Consulting Group, Inc. International copyrights reserved in all countries. No part of this book may be reproduced in any form without written permission from the publisher. The Essential Library™ is a trademark and logo of ABDO Publishing Company.

Printed in the United States of America, North Mankato, Minnesota
112010
012011

Editor: Melissa York
Copy Editor: Amy E. Quale
Interior Design and Production: Christa Schneider
Cover Design: Christa Schneider

Library of Congress Cataloging-in-Publication Data
Grayson, Robert, 1951-
  The Amistad / by Robert Grayson.
    p. cm. -- (Essential events)
  Includes bibliographical references and index.
  ISBN 978-1-61714-761-6
  1. Slave insurrections--United States--Juvenile literature.
2. Amistad (Schooner)--Juvenile literature. 3. Antislavery
movements--United States--Juvenile literature. 4. Slave trade--
America--History. I. Title.
  E447.G73 2011
  326--dc22

                        2010044662

TABLE OF CONTENTS

Slave fortresses such as this one in Ghana dot the coast of West Africa.

IN FREEDOM'S WAKE

The saga began in the morning on a day in early 1839. A 25-year-old rice farmer was kidnapped as he walked on a dusty road in the village of Mani. Kidnappings were not unusual in this West African region, called Mendeland. The rice farmer was known in his village as Sengbe Pieh, but history would record his name as Joseph Cinqué. The four men who snatched him away from Mani wanted to make the farmer into a slave. The kidnappers marched Cinqué to Lomboko, which was a slave fortress in Sierra Leone, a British colony at the time. Great Britain had banned the slave trade in 1807, but illegal trading continued.

Once at Lomboko, Cinqué sat in a cell for more than two months. He waited as kidnappers captured enough of his fellow Africans to fill a ship for the voyage across the Atlantic to the Americas. Kidnappers traded their human captives for goods such as cotton, alcohol, and guns.

Slave trading was the act of illegally taking people from their homeland, mainly Africa, and bringing them to other countries to be sold into slavery. In 1839, slave trading had been against the laws of Spain for 22 years. Portugal had outlawed slave trading north of the equator in 1815. However, neither country vigorously enforced the laws.

Lomboko

The slave fortress Lomboko, run by Pedro Blanco, operated on the coast of Sierra Leone, a British colony in West Africa. Blanco became a slave trader around 1822. He ran Lomboko like a private kingdom. He shipped out thousands of kidnapped Africans each year to be sold as slaves, even after slave trading was banned. In 1849, ten years after Joseph Cinqué was held in Lomboko, the British Royal Navy launched a surprise attack on the fortress, completely destroying it.

INHUMANE CONDITIONS

Once enough Africans had been illegally taken from their villages, they were packed tightly onto slave ships for the Middle Passage, the voyage to the Americas. In late April 1839, Cinqué, together with hundreds of his fellow kidnapped Africans, was put on the Portuguese slave ship *Teçora*. They were bound for Cuba, which was a Spanish colony at the time. Because of the crude conditions aboard the *Teçora*, about a third of the Africans died during the two-month trip to Havana. The air was foul below deck where the Africans were kept. Food and water were in short supply. The enslaved Africans became ill and the stench of death surrounded the captives. Those Africans who died during the long trip to the Americas were simply thrown overboard.

Even though slave trading was banned by the United States and most of Europe by this time, the abhorrent practice of slavery was still

The Middle Passage

Between the sixteenth and early nineteenth centuries, the triangular trade route brought millions of kidnapped Africans across the Atlantic to the New World to be traded as slaves. During the first leg of the trip, ships traveled from Europe to Africa, leaving Europe loaded with commercial goods to be traded for kidnapped Africans. The Middle Passage was the second leg of the Atlantic slave trade route, when the Africans would be taken to the New World to be traded for raw materials. In the final leg, raw materials from the New World were transported back to Europe, where they were turned into commercial goods.

Conditions on the Amistad *would have been similar to those on this illegal slave ship from 1860.*

legal in some countries, including the United States and Cuba. While Spain looked the other way, Cuba even continued the practice of slave trading, making it a thriving illegal business within its borders.

The *Teçora* arrived in Havana on an afternoon in June, but it did not dock until nightfall. The kidnapped Africans were brought ashore under the cover of darkness so no one would know they had just been brought from Africa. As soon as the Africans stepped foot on Cuban soil, the Portuguese and Spanish would claim they were Spanish subjects born in Cuba, not victims of illegal slave trading.

Once in Cuba, the Africans were given forged identification papers. Their names were changed to reflect a Spanish ancestry. The papers referred to the rice farmer, Sengbe Pieh, as Joseph Cinqué. Several days after they arrived in Cuba, 53 of the Africans who had come to Cuba aboard the *Teçora*—49 men, including Cinqué, and four children— were sold to two Spanish plantation owners, José Ruiz and Pedro Montes. The children, three

A Moral Contradiction

Even though a number of countries adopted laws in the early 1800s to abolish slave trading, many of those same countries failed to outlaw slavery altogether—a clear moral contradiction. Great Britain banned slave trading in 1807 and assigned British ships to patrol the African coast to catch slave traders. Great Britain pressured other European nations to outlaw slave trading as well, including Spain and Portugal. Yet slavery itself still went on within British territories until 1833.

The United States also patrolled the high seas for slave traders, who faced death if they were caught. Yet slavery was not outlawed within US borders until passage of the Thirteenth Amendment to the US Constitution in 1865.

While Spain banned slavery in 1811 at home, it was sanctioned in the Spanish colonies of Cuba until 1886 and Puerto Rico until 1873. Some of the countries that banned slave trading were also very lax in enforcing those laws. Spanish officials in Cuba who witnessed a ship bringing Africans into the colony to be traded as slaves, for instance, were easily bribed by the slave traders to look the other way.

girls and one boy, were between the ages of seven and nine. On June 28, shortly after that sale, the Africans were put on a schooner called *La Amistad,* which set sail for Puerto Principe, Cuba, on the other side of the island. Ironically, *amistad* means "friendship" in Spanish.

Schooners were fast sailing ships, and the trip to Puerto Principe should have taken only two days. The schooner's crew consisted of Captain Ramon Ferrer, a cook, and two other sailors. Captain Ferrer's cabin boy, a slave named Antonio, was also onboard, as were Ruiz and Montes. Unexpected rain and wind gusts prolonged the trip, which entered its third day still far from its destination.

Making Their Move

Cinqué and the other captives were treated cruelly. On the *Amistad,* a thirsty captive was whipped for drinking too much water. The Africans were determined to try to escape from captivity if they got the chance. Speaking Mende, their native

Spark for Revolt

Celestino, the cook on the *Amistad,* added to the anxiety of the Africans aboard the schooner, making them only more determined to take over the ship. On the first day of the trip, he made a crude joke. He motioned to Cinqué that the Africans' throats were going to be slit. Then he made gestures that the dead Africans would be cut up and eaten. Thinking that certain death loomed, the Mende men felt they had nothing to lose by staging a revolt.

language, Cinqué told the other captives, "If we do nothing, we be killed. We may as well die in trying to be free."[1]

The Africans were kept chained below deck on the *Amistad*, but they were brought topside once a day to exercise. While exercising, the Africans were heavily guarded by the ship's crew. On July 1, 1839, the fourth day at sea, when Cinqué was exercising in the open air, he noticed a loose nail sticking out of a wood plank. With one cleverly calculated motion, he pulled the nail out of the plank with his chained hands and hurriedly concealed it under his armpit.

That night, stormy weather once again roiled the waters around Cuba. The crew of the *Amistad* spent most of the night trying to keep the schooner afloat amid the fierce winds of the storm. No one was guarding the Africans. The crew did not feel it was

Second in Command

In Lomboko, Cinqué was held in a cell next to Grabeau, another Mende rice farmer. The two men did not know each other in Mendeland, but they became close friends while in the Lomboko fortress. Fate would keep them together throughout the entire *Amistad* episode. Cinqué and Grabeau were both on the *Teçora*. The two men were bought by José Ruiz in Cuba and put on the *Amistad.* When Cinqué led the *Amistad* rebellion, he asked Grabeau to be his second in command. Cinqué relied heavily on his friend for guidance and showed the same support in return.

necessary because no slaves had ever gotten free of their chains before.

The noise from the storm gave the Africans the perfect cover to move around without being heard. With the help of one of the other captives who had been a blacksmith in Mendeland, Cinqué used the nail he had taken from the deck to unlock his chains. Then, with the same nail, Cinqué released his fellow captives. Once freed, the Africans looked for weapons. They knew the crew was armed with guns and would use them. As they searched the lower deck, the Africans found a box of machetes, the large knives used to cut down sugarcane.

At about 4:00 a.m. on July 2, when the seas were finally calmed down, there was a hush over the deck. All but one member of the crew had finally bunked down for the night. The remaining crew member was steering the ship. From below deck, the Africans quietly climbed up a ladder, swung open the hatch, and jumped on deck. They made their way toward the sailor steering the ship. The sailor spotted the group of men heading toward him and started yelling. The rest of the *Amistad* crew, still weary from battling the storm, awakened and came running to his aid.

Africa's Role

Cinqué's kidnappers were four African men. At the height of slave trading in the New World, Africans regularly sold or traded members of rival tribes to slave traders. Some tribes exchanged prisoners captured in battle for supplies from the New World. Others kidnapped members of rival villages and swapped them for goods with slave traders. Some who kidnapped Africans from their villages worked directly for the slave traders.

A Fight for Freedom

A brutal fight broke out. Shots were fired and flashed in the darkness. Screams could be heard as bullets struck or whistled by some of the captives. The cook wildly swung a large kitchen knife. Machetes were flailing. The two sailors threw a rowboat into the water and jumped overboard. The cook was killed in the fight, as was Captain Ferrer.

The Africans were now in control of the *Amistad*. In the rebellion, one African was killed; the slave owners—Montes and Ruiz—were both captured by the Africans. Montes was injured in the uprising, but Ruiz was unhurt. For the moment, the Africans had gained their freedom.

This depiction of the death of Captain Ferrer appeared
in contemporary newspapers.

This modern replica of the Amistad *periodically retraces the original ship's route.*

High Stakes on the High Seas

ow in control of the *Amistad,* Cinqué's fervent hope was to get back to Africa. However, the slave owners Montes and Ruiz had been captured by the Africans and were still aboard the schooner. They were hoping a Spanish or

US ship would pass by and rescue them. For both sides, the stakes were high.

For the Africans, Montes and Ruiz were valuable men to have on the *Amistad*. None of the Africans had any sailing experience, but the two Spaniards did. Gesturing, Cinqué ordered the two men to sail in the direction of the rising sun, toward Mendeland. During his voyage to Cuba, the kidnapped rice farmer had seen the *Teçora* head toward the setting sun. He concluded—correctly—that the way home was in the opposite direction.

Instead of following Cinqué's orders, however, the two cunning plantation owners took advantage of the Africans' lack of nautical knowledge. They sailed east during the day as Cinqué had instructed, but with the sails hardly catching the wind. At night, they headed northwest with the sails fully angled to the wind. In that way, the *Amistad* followed a zigzag pattern up the Atlantic Coast, never getting any closer to the Africans' homeland. During the journey, the *Amistad* also ran into storms. Each encounter with severe weather left the ship more battered than before, the sails torn, tattered, and less seaworthy.

Food and water were running low. On several occasions, the *Amistad* passed other ships. When that happened, Cinqué ordered Montes and Ruiz below deck and traded for food and water with the other vessels. Sailors on the other ships did not know what to make of the ragtag crew on the *Amistad*. Rumors started to circulate that a group of black pirates was sailing on the high seas.

The End of the Voyage

Though Montes and Ruiz were aware that slave trading was outlawed in the United States, they knew that slavery itself was not. Therefore, they believed if they came across a US ship, they would be rescued and the Africans would be recaptured.

Meanwhile, harsh conditions on the *Amistad* were claiming lives. Some of the Africans became ill from the lack of fresh food or from drinking salt water. Others became sick or died from overdosing on liquid medicines onboard the ship, which they drank when freshwater was unavailable.

Father Figure

Throughout the *Amistad's* voyage, Cinqué looked out for the well-being of the four children—three girls and a boy. He kept them out of the fighting during the rebellion aboard the ship. When food was running low aboard the *Amistad*, Cinqué gave his portion to the children.

In late August, nearly 60 days since the Africans took over the *Amistad*, Cinqué ordered the ship to head for land. Thirty-nine of the African men and all four children survived the ordeal. Ten African men had died since the ship left Cuba.

Supplies were now dangerously low. Many aboard the ship were weak and hungry. When the *Amistad* came within view of land, Cinqué and several of the other Africans took a rowboat from the ship and went ashore. Montes and Ruiz had led them to Culloden Point on Long Island, New York.

Once they reached land, the Africans met people who were willing to trade food and water for gold coins Cinqué had brought with him from the *Amistad*. At the same time, the USS *Washington,* a vessel of the US Navy, was on a routine mission off the Long Island coast. The *Washington*'s commander, Lieutenant Thomas R. Gedney, spotted the weathered *Amistad* and thought something was amiss. He had heard the reports of the black pirate ship, so he ordered his men to investigate.

Lieutenant Richard Meade led a group of sailors in rowboats from the *Washington* to the wayward ship. When Cinqué saw the men in uniforms going toward the *Amistad,* he left the shore immediately and headed quickly back to the schooner. He arrived too late. The ship had been boarded by the US Navy. The sailors were armed with guns, and the Africans were too weak to put up a fight.

A One-Sided Story

Meade asked the Africans to show him the ship's documents, but none of them understood what the sailors were saying. Meade did speak Spanish, however. Montes and Ruiz were quick to tell the US sailors their story about how the Africans had rebelled aboard the schooner.

Risky Encounter

Cinqué's decision to leave the *Amistad* and go ashore to find food and water was necessary but very risky. The *Amistad* Africans were in dire need of provisions, but he did not know where he was or whom to trust. Although some people came out of their homes and traded a few items with the unexpected visitors, most stayed away. Henry Green, a sea captain, was one of the few who made contact with Cinqué.

Green saw Cinqué row ashore, and he decided to approach the stranger. Cinqué offered to trade some gold coins for food and water. Green had other ideas. Seeing the gold Cinqué was ready to exchange for supplies, Green reasoned that there must be more gold and other items of great value hidden on the anchored *Amistad*. He figured he could get the valuables by seizing the ship. Green tried to convince Cinqué to invite him and his fellow sailors aboard, but the African declined. Green then tried to entice Cinqué to bring the rest of the Africans ashore, but Cinqué again declined. Cinqué became suspicious of Green's repeated attempts to separate the Africans from their ship. He kept Green away from the ship while trade talks proceeded. The US Navy arrived before Green could pull off his plan.

The Spaniards failed to mention anything about the Africans' illegal kidnapping.

Meade relayed the Spaniards' story to his commander. Despite hearing only one side of the story, Gedney decided to arrest the Africans and tow the *Amistad* to the port in New London, Connecticut. The decision to go to Connecticut was a deliberate move by Gedney, who was aware that slavery was allowed in Connecticut but outlawed in New York. Gedney was hoping that when the matter of the *Amistad* was sorted out, he and his crew would receive a reward for recovering the ship's contents. He assumed the amount of the reward would be based on the total value of the cargo, including the Africans. Whether the Africans were considered property with a price tag or free human beings would become one of the central issues of the *Amistad* case.

Born to Lead

At 25 years old, Cinqué was an imposing figure. He was taller than the other Africans on the *Amistad,* standing roughly six feet eight inches (1.7 m). Most of the other men were approximately 5 feet (1.5 m) tall. Cinqué had a powerful build and was very agile. Married with three children, he was a stable member of his Mende community. His father was a leader in the village where Cinqué lived. Had he not been kidnapped, the young rice farmer would have eventually taken over his father's leadership role.

Fierce Clothing

The cargo aboard the *Amistad* included colorful silks and satins. The Africans fashioned clothing from these materials once they took command of the ship. The brightly colored garb, plus the long sugarcane knives the Africans carried as weapons, created quite a sight. The *Amistad* passed a number of other ships during its two-month voyage up the East Coast. Most of those ships steered clear of the schooner once crew members saw the Africans dressed in such unusual and frightening outfits.

FALSE REPORTS

Once the USS *Washington* took charge of the *Amistad,* the story started getting a great deal of attention in the press. Some of the initial news reports were completely wrong; others contained some accurate information. The most common error in the press was that the *Amistad* had been taken over by black pirates who killed the ship's captain and crew. Reporters went on to write that if the pirates had not been captured, they had planned to attack other ships.

Nothing could have been further from the truth. Eventually, the true story of the *Amistad* Africans' kidnapping and illegal transport to the Americas would come out. Some newspapers would make the case that slave trading was outlawed in the United States and, therefore, the Africans should be freed. As the nation debated their fate, the *Amistad* Africans would be held against their will.

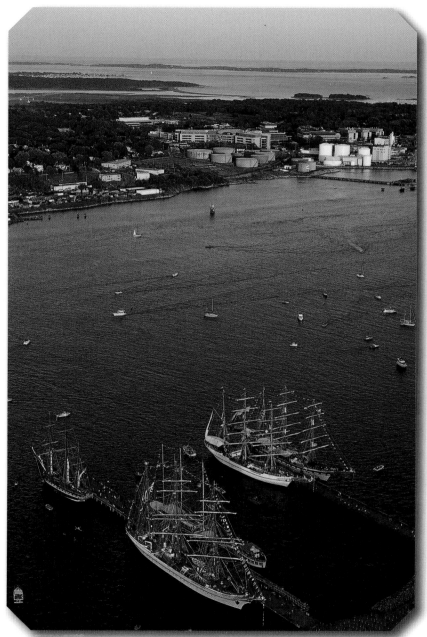

A modern view of the harbor in New London, Connecticut

The framers of the US Constitution hotly debated the issue of slavery.

AWAKENING A NATION'S CONSCIENCE

Word spread that the *Amistad* was being towed into New London. Crowds gathered to see the ship brought into port. The ships arrived on August 27, 1839, and Lieutenant Gedney turned the ship over to federal authorities.

Within hours of the *Amistad*'s arrival in New London, a federal district judge and a US marshal were ordered to New London. The federal district judge was Andrew T. Judson and the US marshal was Norris Wilcox, and they were both based in New Haven, Connecticut. It was Judson's job to determine what should be done with the ship, its cargo, and the 43 Africans, all now in US custody. Judson scheduled a hearing aboard the *Washington* on August 29.

The Africans' plight made them celebrities in New London, throughout New England, and in parts of New York. Once translators were found and newspaper reporters discovered and reported the true story of the *Amistad,* the saga of the *Amistad* Africans sparked debate throughout the country. When stories appeared in reputable newspapers, stating that the Africans had been

Rousing Oratory

On two occasions after the crew of the USS *Washington* seized the *Amistad,* Cinqué spoke to the other Africans on the schooner. He spoke in his native tongue, and crew members of the *Washington* did not understand what he said. But they noticed that Cinqué's words and tone inspired the Africans. After the second address, Lieutenant Gedney concluded that Cinqué was a dangerous man who might lead another mutiny. So he chained the kidnapped rice farmer and kept him aboard the *Washington,* separate from his fellow Africans on the *Amistad.*

enslaved, it raised a very complex issue for the United States. When the full story finally came out— that the Africans had been victims of the outlawed slave trade—it would complicate the issue even more.

The Slavery Dilemma

In the United States, slavery had been a dilemma as far back as colonial times. Even then, slavery presented both moral and ethical dilemmas. When writing the US Constitution, the nation's founders wrestled with the issue of slavery but could not do away with the practice, even though many of them had just fought a war for their own independence from Great Britain. The forcible enslavement of human beings sparked angry political debate that lasted for decades until the American Civil War (1861–1865).

John Jay, the renowned statesman and the first chief justice of the US Supreme Court, was a leading opponent of slavery. Jay wrote in a letter in 1786, a year before the US Constitution was written:

> *It is much to be wished that slavery may be abolished. The honour of the United States, as well as justice and humanity, in my opinion, loudly call upon them to emancipate these unhappy people. To contend for our own liberty, and to*

US Supreme Court Chief Justice John Jay was an early believer in abolition.

deny that blessing to others, involves an inconsistency not to be excused.[1]

Early members of the US government made a point of limiting slavery. Congress banned slavery in the nation's Northwest Territory when it was created in 1787. When the US Constitution was ratified in 1789, it did not outlaw slavery, even though the issue was the subject of heated debate.

The Northwest Ordinance

Under the Northwest Ordinance of 1787, the Ohio River became the boundary line between free and slave territory from the Appalachian Trail to the Mississippi River. By the 1830s, slavery had been eliminated in most of the northeastern United States. These northeastern states, combined with the new states in the Northwest Territory, made up a connected region of free states. This shifted the balance of congressional power from the slave states in the South to the free states in the North. It strengthened the voice of those seeking an end to slavery.

Faced with the threat that the young nation might divide over the volatile issue, the Constitution's writers made compromises in the document that kept slavery legal. In addition, Congress agreed not to end slave trading until after 1808. In the United States, slavery was practiced mostly in the South and would continue until the American Civil War brought it to a violent end in 1865.

COUNTERING SLAVERY

For decades before the American Civil War, a group of people known as abolitionists worked hard to abolish, or bring an end to, slavery. By 1839, the abolition movement was growing strong in the North. Still, the abolitionists needed to stir up popular and political support for the drive to end slavery. Seeing the spirited debate sparked by the *Amistad* Africans, many abolitionists believed they had found the case they needed to get courts in the United States to rule against slavery once and for all. The *Amistad* case gave the abolition movement a way to highlight the immorality of slavery.

By spotlighting the *Amistad* case, abolitionists were determined to prove that not only was slave trading still going on but that it was also big business. Abolitionists would publicly call attention to kidnapped Africans, like those on the *Amistad*, being smuggled into the Americas. As slaves, the

Two Abolition Movements

The abolition movement in the United States had two distinct factions. One group of abolitionists wanted to see slavery ended gradually. The other wanted slavery stopped immediately, even if violence became necessary to accomplish the goal. The *Amistad* case unfolded at a time when abolitionists in both factions were making a major push to end slavery. Many abolitionists felt that slavery was a symbol for everything that was wrong in US society. The abolitionists printed antislavery newspapers and helped runaway slaves gain their freedom. Those who favored slavery pushed back, going so far as to physically attack antislavery activists, break into their meetings, start fistfights with them, and even damage their homes.

Many Northerners opposed slavery, but they thought that the abolitionists were too radical. They felt the abolitionists' uncompromising attitude was bad for the nation's economy as a whole and would eventually split the Union.

The *Amistad* issue and the debate it raised divided the nation's newspapers. Once details of the Africans' plight became known, mostly Northern, abolitionist newspapers referred to Joseph Cinqué as a brave leader and a hero. Proslavery periodicals, however, called the Africans aboard the *Amistad* rebellious murderers. The battle lines over slavery were clearly drawn.

Africans were deprived of their basic civil and human rights. The abolitionists would challenge whether slaves were people or, as slave owners claimed, property. Although they did not realize it at first, the *Amistad* Africans had found a corps of determined allies.

A Historic Hearing

Judge Judson held a hearing aboard the *Washington* on August 29, 1839, to start the process of determining what to do with the contents of the ship. This hearing attracted a number of onlookers who believed they were witnessing history. The judge took testimony from the Spanish slave owners Montes and Ruiz, as well as Antonio, the slave who had been owned by Captain Ferrer. Montes and Ruiz told their story about how the Africans had taken over the ship. They argued that the *Amistad* and all its cargo, including the Africans, should be turned over to the Spanish consul in Boston, Massachusetts. Judson examined the ship's papers and found that the *Amistad* was indeed a Spanish slave transport ship. The papers stated that the ship was operating legally under Spanish law, carrying 53 Latino slaves from Havana to Puerto Principe. Although 53 Africans—49 men and four children—began the trip aboard the *Amistad,* one of the men died in the uprising and nine more men died during the voyage to Long Island, leaving 39 men and the four children aboard the ship when the *Amistad* was seized.

Cinqué was briefly brought before the judge but could not speak for himself because of the language barrier. The Africans had no translator and no lawyer to represent them yet.

Judson decided to detain the 39 African men until the next meeting of the grand jury of the US circuit court. The grand jury would meet in Hartford, Connecticut, on September 17. Property claims would be decided at that time. The grand jury would also determine if the Africans would stand trial for murder and mutiny. Judson did determine that the four African children aboard the *Amistad* did not take part in the

In the New Haven Jail

After the hearing on the *Washington* ended, the entire group of Africans from the *Amistad* was taken to the New Haven jail. Cinqué was put in a holding cell with common criminals. The rest of the Africans were held in a barracks-like setting. Because none of the Africans spoke English, they did not know the outcome of the hearing or their fate. They might have thought they were going back to Cuba or worried they had been sentenced to death. One thing they knew for sure: they were not free.

Medical Aid

After spending two months at sea, many of the Africans who survived their experience onboard the *Amistad* were in need of medical treatment. Harsh weather conditions, poor diet, lack of water, and the stress of the situation made many of the Africans ill. The abolitionists brought in doctors to examine the survivors and give them any health care they needed. Several of the men were close to death, but they were nursed back to health once they reached New London.

mutiny and would not be brought up on any charges relating to the rebellion at sea. The question of whose property they were remained open. However, they were ordered to the New Haven jail with the other Africans. They would be called upon to serve as witnesses when the adults went to trial.

Abolitionist Dwight P. Janes attended the hearing and had no doubt that the Africans were not Spanish subjects. He also knew that Montes and Ruiz had lied about the birthplace of the people they referred to as their property.

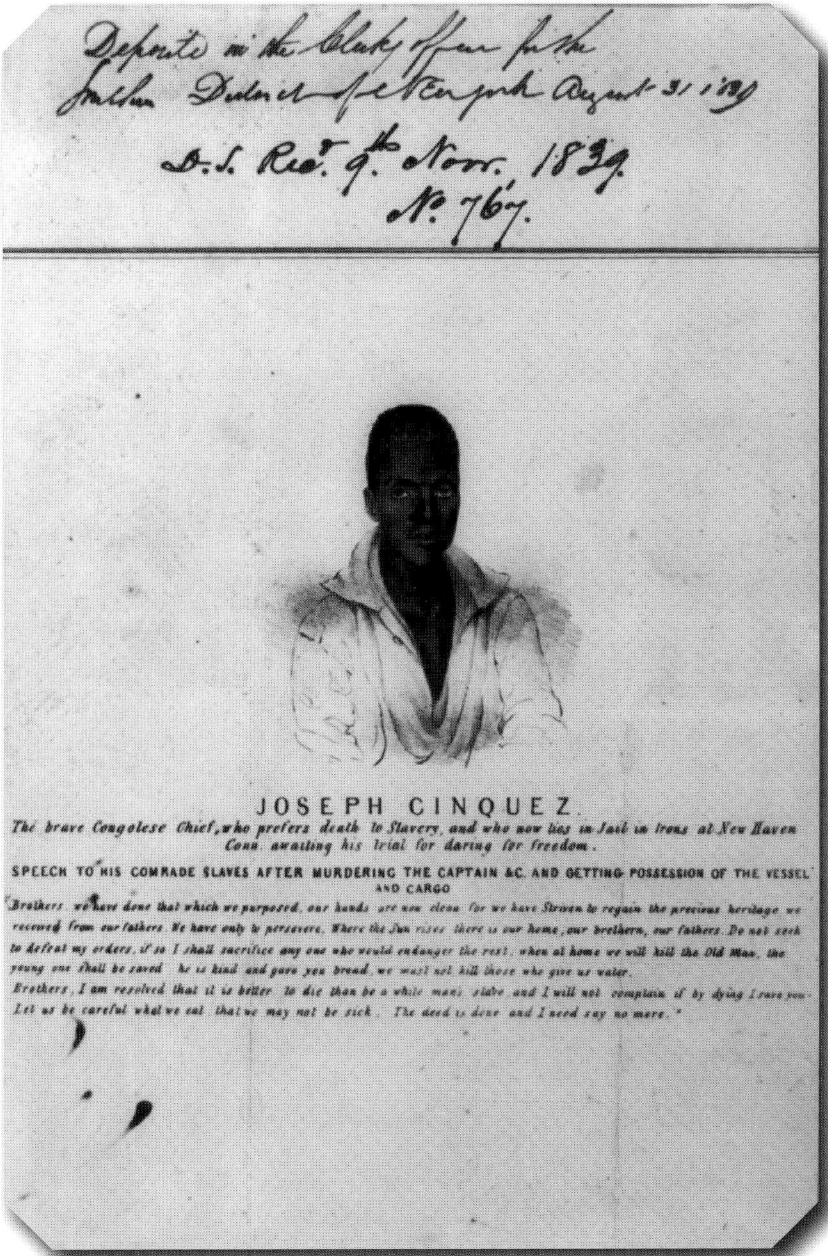

Deposited in the Clerk's office for the Southern District of New York August 31 1839

D. S. Recd. 9th Novr. 1839.
No. 767.

JOSEPH CINQUEZ.

The brave Congolese Chief, who prefers death to Slavery, and who now lies in Jail in Irons at New Haven Conn. awaiting his trial for daring for freedom.

SPEECH TO HIS COMRADE SLAVES AFTER MURDERING THE CAPTAIN &C. AND GETTING POSSESSION OF THE VESSEL AND CARGO

"Brothers we have done that which we purposed, our hands are now clean for we have Striven to regain the precious heritage we received from our fathers. We have only to persevere, Where the Sun rises there is our home, our brethern, our fathers. Do not seek to defeat my orders, if so I shall sacrifice any one who would endanger the rest, when at home we will kill the Old Man, the young one shall be saved he is kind and gave you bread, we must not kill those who give us water.

Brothers, I am resolved that it is better to die than be a white mans slave, and I will not complain if by dying I save you. Let us be careful what we eat that we may not be sick. The deed is done and I need say no more."

Sympathetic images and reports about the Amistad captives helped win public opinion to their side.

Chapter

4

Lewis Tappan was a well-known US abolitionist who funded antislavery protests around the country.

RALLYING SUPPORT

When Dwight P. Janes attended the August 29, 1839, hearing for the *Amistad* defendants on the USS *Washington,* he never revealed that he was an ardent abolitionist. He arrived at the hearing early and looked for Ruiz.

Ruiz spoke some English. Upon finding Ruiz waiting for the hearing to start, Janes engaged the Spaniard in a conversation. Janes eventually brought up the question he was most interested in—the language issue.

After the hearing, Janes sent a letter to Reverend Josiah Leavitt, a leading New York abolitionist. Janes wrote, "I inquired if they [the *Amistad* Africans] could speak Spanish. He [Ruiz] said no, they were just from Africa."[1] The impact of that statement was not lost on either Janes or Leavitt, another prominent abolitionist. It meant the Africans were not Spanish subjects at all. They had been victims of the illegal slave trade.

ORGANIZING FOR THE FIGHT AHEAD

Abolitionists got busy as soon as the hearing on the *Washington* was over. Antislavery activists throughout Connecticut were already building a network of support for the *Amistad* defendants. With Janes's letter in hand, the New York abolitionists were ready to join the fight.

Leavitt enlisted the support of activist Lewis Tappan, a wealthy New York businessman, to form a committee to help the *Amistad* defendants. They also asked Simeon S. Jocelyn, a New Haven minister, to fill out the group of three who would run their legal team, known as the Amistad Committee.

By September 4, the three men had organized the Amistad Committee and had started raising funds for the defense and other needs of the imprisoned Africans from the *Amistad*. The committee's first flyer appealing for funds to help the Africans said they had been "piratically kidnapped from their native land, transported across the seas, and subjected to atrocious cruelties."[2] Money from supporters began pouring in.

Assembling a Legal Team

Meanwhile, the group needed to assemble a legal team to represent Cinqué and his fellow Africans. Janes lobbied fellow abolitionists to ask New Haven attorney Roger Sherman Baldwin to lead the defense. Baldwin had a reputation for taking on difficult cases and representing the less fortunate. Shortly after he started practicing law in Connecticut in 1814, Baldwin championed the case of a runaway slave and won the man's freedom. Baldwin also stood up against a New Haven mob in 1831 when he supported a plan to build a black college near Yale College.

Baldwin was an outstanding orator and a man of high principle. He made his courtroom arguments with great passion because he believed in the causes for which he advocated. Baldwin was the ideal attorney for the *Amistad* Africans, and he agreed to take the case. He thought justice was so important in the case that he declared he was not certain he would even charge for his legal services.

The abolitionists believed the *Amistad* case required extensive preparation—more than one attorney could handle. So they next asked for the help of Seth Staples. Staples had attended Yale College in New Haven and now practiced law in New York City. Staples agreed to accept nothing but expense money for his work on the *Amistad* defense team.

In the same New York City building where Staples had his legal practice was the law office of another highly skilled lawyer. Theodore

Longtime Visionary

Simeon Jocelyn was the first white pastor of an all-black church in New Haven. He had been battling slavery since the early 1820s. In 1831, Jocelyn went to Philadelphia to attend the first Convention of the Free People of Colour. At that convention, Jocelyn talked about his idea for an all-black college in New Haven. But Yale elites and New Haven politicians blocked Jocelyn's efforts, and the idea died. Jocelyn never stopped fighting for racial justice. He and his brother, Nathaniel, were volunteers with the Underground Railroad and helped hundreds of fugitive slaves escape to the North.

Sedgwick was an antislavery supporter whose legal skills impressed Lewis Tappan. With the permission of the rest of the Amistad Committee, Tappan asked Sedgwick to join the defense team as well. The energetic Sedgwick was eager to lend his talents to the cause.

Within just a few days, the Amistad Committee had put together a committed, polished, and impressive legal group to build the Africans' defense. The abolitionists also felt this legal team could use the *Amistad* case to mount one of the most serious assaults on slavery ever seen in the United States.

Overcoming the Language Barrier

Tappan was well aware that advocates for the *Amistad* Africans had to find a way to speak to the defendants. While helping put together the legal team, Tappan began a search to find African natives living in New York City who could communicate with the Mende men. If the kidnapping victims could give the abolitionists more facts to work with, it would make their case stronger. It would also help to contradict the testimony of Montes and Ruiz. Challenges to the Spaniards' one-sided account of events aboard the *Amistad* would be weak as long as the Africans could not tell their side of the story in court.

If they could communicate with Cinqué and his fellow Africans, the abolitionists would also be able to publicize more details about their ordeal since leaving Africa. Even with what little was known about Cinqué's fight for freedom aboard the *Amistad*, he had become a hero in the

Committed to the Cause

Abolitionist brothers Lewis and Arthur Tappan, relatives of Benjamin Franklin, were wealthy New York City businessmen. They had little patience for those who supported slavery, either by keeping slaves themselves or by doing nothing to stop it. The brothers used their money to battle slavery at all levels, funding trials for runaway slaves, supporting schools for African Americans, and starting and funding abolitionist newspapers and organizations.

Those who opposed their efforts were not shy either. They vandalized the offices where the Tappans worked, broke into the brothers' homes, and sent the pair threatening letters. In the mid-1830s, a group of Southerners who supported slavery offered a $100,000 reward for anyone who delivered the bodies of Lewis and Arthur Tappan to a slave state. Because of the threats of violence and the actual vandalism against their property, no insurance company would cover anything owned by the Tappans. The brothers never backed down, however. Lewis even refused to arm himself with anything but the New Testament of the Bible, believing he was carrying out God's work.

newspapers. Cinqué was the face of people fighting the evils of slavery everywhere in the United States. The abolitionists knew they were winning the hearts of the public. The Northern newspapers were solidly on the side of the Africans. Few reporters believed Cinqué and his fellow defendants were Cuban natives.

Tappan found three African men living in New York City who could speak English as well as various languages from their homelands. One of the three men was John Ferry. Ferry himself had been kidnapped from Africa when he was only 12 years old. He had been taken to the northwestern part of South America, where he was enslaved. He was freed when Simon Bolivar liberated the region in 1819. Tappan rushed the three men to New Haven, hoping that at least one of them could communicate with the *Amistad* defendants. Communicating with the men would be vital to freeing them. ⌐

Roger Sherman Baldwin represented the Africans
in the historic Amistad trials.

Proslavery advocates worried the Amistad *trials could throw the whole institution of slavery into question.*

STRATEGIC MOVES

The *Amistad* case would affect more than just the defendants. Proslavery activists feared that a verdict in favor of the *Amistad* defendants would lead to slave revolts and undermine the institution of slavery in the United States. Meanwhile, Spanish officials were pressuring the United States to turn over the *Amistad* and all its cargo to Spain, including the Africans, under the terms of a treaty the two countries had signed in 1795 and renewed in 1819.

As lawyers prepared the Africans' defense and domestic and international issues simmered, communication remained a problem. The three men Tappan brought to New Haven to speak with the *Amistad* Africans were having little success. Ferry did make some progress, however. He spoke the African languages of Mandingo and Gallinao, but most of the captives spoke only Mende. Three of the children, however, did speak Mandingo. Ferry was able to determine that they had been kidnapped in Africa and illegally brought to Cuba. This was not much, but it proved the validity of the abolitionists' case. Still, more was needed.

A Communication Breakthrough

Hearing about the communication problem, Josiah W. Gibbs, a linguistics expert at Yale College, visited the Africans in New Haven. He asked the Africans to teach him some numbers in the Mende language. He then went to the New Haven and New York City waterfronts, where many Africans worked. He yelled out the numbers, hoping someone would recognize the language and respond. Two men did—James Covey and Charles Pratt, both from the Mende region of West Africa. Both men spoke and understood Mende as well as English.

Gibbs brought the two men to visit the Africans in the New Haven jail. Because most of the *Amistad* Africans were from Mendeland, they lit up when they heard their native language being spoken. After hearing partial accounts of what the jailed Africans had been through, Covey agreed to stay for as long as he was needed. Pratt had to return to the waterfront at the end of the day. The interpreters confirmed what most already suspected: the Africans were victims of an outlawed slave trading enterprise in Cuba.

Covey managed to help in many ways. He listened to detailed statements from the Africans about

James Covey's Story

James Covey was 24 years old when he encountered Josiah Gibbs on the New York City waterfront. Seven years earlier, Covey had been kidnapped in his native Sierra Leone and put on a slave ship bound for Cuba. A British patrol ship seized the illegal slave ship and set Covey free. Covey settled in Britain, learned English, and then took to the sea as a sailor. He happened to be in New York City at just the right time to encounter Gibbs. He became a lifeline for the Africans in the *Amistad* case.

With help from translators, the Amistad *lawyers were able to confirm that the Africans had been kidnapped into slavery.*

how they ended up in Cuba and on the *Amistad*. He assisted students from Yale in teaching the Africans English and adjusting to life as prisoners in the United States. He eased the Africans' fears and would become a strong witness for the defense. As the story emerged in the Africans' own words, it became clear the Africans were kidnap victims who had a right to freedom.

INTERNATIONAL INTRIGUE

Nothing could have been worse for Spain than Covey's arrival. However, Spain was not going to back down on its demands. The Spanish were hoping to get the schooner and the Africans returned to their custody quickly. The Spanish were claiming the Africans had been born in Cuba. They wanted to put the captives on trial for murder and piracy charges in their own courts. In their view, that was the only way they could prevent similar uprisings from happening again.

The abolitionists, meanwhile, accused the Spanish of a plot to convict the Africans of piracy and sentence them to death before Spain could be linked to the illegal slave-trading business. Meanwhile, the Spanish government seemed intent on using the *Amistad* as a test of the relationship between Spain and the United States, pressuring the

Headed for the United States

Some US abolitionists did not believe the slave traders intended for the Africans aboard the *Amistad* to end up in Cuba. Ruiz paid $450 apiece for each of the 49 adult African males he purchased in Havana. Members of the antislavery movement asserted that men such as Ruiz purchased the Africans to smuggle them to the South in the United States. Once there, the Africans would be sold to Southern plantation owners at a large profit.

US government to honor treaties between the two countries.

Added to the political intrigue was the fact that President Martin Van Buren was facing reelection in 1840. Van Buren could not win without Southern votes and did not want to do anything that would make him appear as though he were opposed to slavery. Pressure from Spain and from the proslavery activists was forcing the Van Buren administration to confront the issue. The more Van Buren tried to ignore the *Amistad* issue, the more the two groups demanded he take a stand.

Angel Calderon de la Barca, the Spanish minister in Washington DC, was quick to cite Pinckney's Treaty of 1795 as grounds for the return of the *Amistad* with all its cargo, including the Africans—no questions asked. According to Calderon, the treaty's terms went into effect if a ship was diverted because of "stress of weather,

Walking a Fine Line

Martin Van Buren, a New Yorker, needed a united Democratic Party to win reelection. The party could only stay united as long as the issue of slavery was set aside. Van Buren himself remained neutral on the issue and avoided addressing it at all costs. For the sake of the 1840 election the president had two goals regarding the *Amistad*: he wanted to avoid any confrontation with Spain that would test his foreign policy skills, and he wanted to steer clear of the slavery issue.

pursuit of pirates or enemies, or any other urgent necessity." Calderon added that the treaty said the ship "shall [in] no ways be hindered from returning out of the said ports."[1]

Based on that interpretation of the treaty, Calderon said the US courts had no jurisdiction over the *Amistad* Africans because they were Spanish subjects. That would leave the matter up to the Spanish courts. He argued that the US Navy had simply rescued the *Amistad* from the hands of savages. Under the terms of the treaty, following a

No Investigation

The Van Buren administration did not investigate the *Amistad* case with its own lawyers. This opened the administration to criticism, even from those only mildly opposed to slavery. Administration lawyers did not seek out any information from Cuban officials. They did not collect their own evidence. The administration did not try to find out if the *Amistad* regularly transported slaves. Van Buren's people did not attempt to determine if slave trading was going on in Cuba and, if it was, whether Spanish officials were aware of it. No background checks were done on Montes or Ruiz to see if they were known slave traders. No one investigated whether Cuba routinely falsified papers for Africans just brought into the country.

The administration argued that Pinckney's Treaty prevented them from investigating the property claims of citizens of Spain—that is, Montes and Ruiz. Because the traders had properly stamped papers from Cuba, the administration contended that it had no legal grounds to investigate. Moreover, because Spain's slave trade was outlawed by a treaty with Great Britain and no trading had taken place on US soil, the United States had no right to intervene. However, legal experts could easily poke holes in these arguments. It was clear the administration was doing everything it could to stop the matter from going to trial.

rescue, the United States was obligated to step aside and turn the matter over to the Spanish government.

SPEAKING FOR THE ADMINISTRATION

John Forsyth, the secretary of state, represented the Van Buren administration. Forsyth had been the nation's minister to Spain from 1819 to 1823. A native of Georgia, he was a slave owner himself and supported slavery. He believed the United States should honor Spain's demand for the return of the *Amistad* and its cargo, including the Africans, or, as he saw it, the Cubans aboard the ship. He did not think US courts had the legal right to decide the case, because in his eyes it involved Spanish people on a Spanish ship.

The abolitionists feared that President Van Buren might try to go around the US legal system. They thought he might issue an executive

No Decision

Andrew Jackson preceded Martin Van Buren as president of the United States, and the two men were close political allies. On several occasions during Jackson's presidency (1829–1837), Governor Sam Houston of Texas, a longtime friend of Jackson's, petitioned to have Texas join the Union. But that raised a thorny question: Should Texas join the Union as a free or a slave state? Supporters on both sides warned that the question threatened to destroy Jackson's presidency. Rather than have that happen, Jackson kept denying requests for Texas to become a state. Van Buren hoped this same strategy of avoidance would work with the *Amistad* case.

order to return the *Amistad* and the captives to Spanish custody. The defense team sent letters to President Van Buren, urging him not to make any independent attempts to honor Spain's claims. Van Buren was caught in the middle of the controversy— exactly where he did not want to end up before the election. ⌐

US president Martin Van Buren did not want to get involved in the
Amistad case while he was facing reelection.

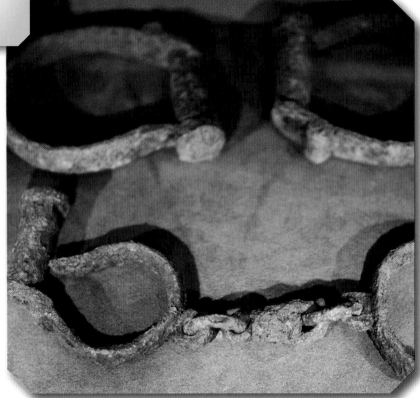

The Amistad *lawyers sought to prove that people could not be property. These shackles were used to hold slaves against their will.*

BUILDING A DEFENSE

here was only one alternative for a president forced to make a decision he did not want to make: let someone else appear to make it. President Van Buren would let a US judge decide whether Spain's claims had merit. He would let the court decide if the Africans on the *Amistad* had been kidnapped. He would also leave it up to a judge to determine if the Africans were people or property. However, leaving the matter up to the courts did not mean Van Buren was bowing out. He would still try to get the verdict he really wanted—an order to return the Africans to the Spanish.

Van Buren knew if the court ruled that the *Amistad* and its cargo, including the Africans, had to be returned to Cuba, he had no choice but to obey the order. If, on the other hand, the court ruled that the *Amistad* defendants were not slaves, he would return them to Africa. Either way, he was doing what the court ordered. He could truthfully claim he had little choice in the matter.

Andrew T. Judson was one of the judges involved in the case. He had been appointed as a federal judge by President Andrew Jackson

Other Countries Demand Action

Officials from Spain threatened to cancel all treaties with the United States if the *Amistad* case was not decided in their favor. The Spanish were determined to get the *Amistad* Africans back in their custody. Meanwhile, Great Britain was demanding action too. British officials called for Spain to prosecute Montes and Ruiz for slave trading. The British were angry and wanted Spain to do something to prove the country was committed to ending slave trading. Spain continued to pursue the *Amistad* case, however.

in 1836. Because Jackson and Van Buren shared many of the same political views, Van Buren felt his administration had nothing to worry about. He did not think it likely the court would rule that the defendants were free individuals. This was a bad miscalculation.

The defendants had some good lawyers, but they also had a secret weapon. The defense team was getting behind-the-scenes legal advice from one of the nation's most prominent attorneys, former president John Quincy Adams. Adams, the nation's sixth president (1825–1829), was an outspoken opponent of slavery. Following his one term as president, he served as a US congressman from Massachusetts. He was serving in Congress during the time of the *Amistad* case.

PEOPLE, NOT PROPERTY

One of the major goals of the defense was to convince the court and the public to think of the defendants simply as people. They wanted to shift the conversation away from viewing the defendants as either slaves or cargo. Rather, they wanted them to be seen as people with rights—the same rights as any free person in the United States.

Former president John Quincy Adams joined the Amistad *legal team.*

In addition, the defense would seek to prove that the Africans were victims of the outlawed slave trade. Because they had been kidnapped, the Africans were taken from their homes against their will. As a result, they had every right to defend themselves and fight for their freedom. The defense would contend that the Africans aboard the *Amistad* were not Cubans, and Montes and Ruiz knew it.

Defense attorney Roger Sherman Baldwin would ask the court for a writ of habeas corpus, the type of court order issued when a person is unlawfully detained. The defense team contended that there was no reason the Africans aboard the *Amistad* should be held in custody. They would argue that the *Amistad* Africans had not committed a crime; rather, they were victims of a crime. The defense would also claim that people could not be held in jail under the assumption that they were property. Because the Africans had been kidnapped, the defense reasoned, they were neither slaves nor property, and they were being held illegally.

Other Legal Issues

Besides murder and piracy charges and the question of whether the Africans were free people or property, the court was asked to rule on a number of other legal matters regarding the *Amistad*:

Lieutenant Gedney was seeking a reward for salvaging the *Amistad*. However, there was some question over whether he had illegally taken the ship from New York to Connecticut in order to face a friendlier court in a slave state.

Captain Green claimed he was entitled to a reward because he deliberately kept Cinqué and some of his men on the Long Island shore. He said he did this in order to give Gedney and his men time to seize the *Amistad*.

Captain Ferrer's family filed papers with the court, demanding the return of the ship itself and Antonio, the enslaved cabin boy.

Various Cuban merchants claimed that they had cargo aboard the ship that was supposed to be delivered to Puerto Principe but never got there. They wanted to be compensated for it.

Baldwin was going to use the circumstances surrounding one nine-year-old defendant, named Kague, to prove this point. She had been sleeping in her parents' home in their native Africa when a group of men broke in and kidnapped the family. The family was split up and sold into slavery. Baldwin, the lead defense attorney, believed that the court should release the little girls who had been aboard the *Amistad* without delay. During the court hearing, he stated:

> *What are the facts? . . . Here are three children between the ages of seven and nine years, who are proved to be native Africans, who cannot speak our language or the Spanish language. . . . Does this honorable court see that they cannot be slaves? They were not born slaves, they were born in Africa. Are we to set aside our own laws, and those of every civilized nation, who have long held this trade to be piratical and infamous?*[1]

Covey Testifies

The Mende interpreter, James Covey, was able to gather details from each of the African detainees about how they had been kidnapped in their homeland, put on a slave ship to Cuba, and eventually ended up on the *Amistad*. He also discovered what the Africans' lives were like in Mendeland—insights about their families and livelihoods. The individual stories helped sketch a profile of each of the Africans. The abolitionists felt those stories made it easier for courtroom spectators and newspaper reporters to relate to the defendants.

Behind the defense arguments was the assertion that the Africans should not and indeed could not be considered property because they were people. This was a pivotal point to the abolitionists. They felt the property issue was the key to ending slavery. If a judicial precedent could be established that human beings were not property, the abolitionists believed it would be a decisive blow to slavery.

A Battle for Freedom

The defense was also looking for reasons to have the hearing moved to a different court. The defense team wanted the case heard in New York where slavery was outlawed, rather than in Connecticut where slavery was still legal. Defense lawyers believed that they would have a more sympathetic ear in New York. They also argued that they had legitimate grounds to move the case, as the *Amistad* was first seized off Long Island, New York. Transferred to another court or not, Baldwin was ready to proceed with the case. He would tell the court that the actions of the Mende men aboard the *Amistad* had not been a crime. He would call their battle for freedom something "every one of us would have done, if placed in similar circumstances."[2]

District Attorney William Holabird would handle the prosecution of the case. A known supporter of slavery, he received orders directly from Secretary of State John Forsyth and Attorney General Felix Grundy. He would represent the Van Buren administration and argue that the defendants should be returned to Spain. To cover all bases, however, Holabird would also ask the court that if they found the Africans had been kidnapped from their homeland, they should be sent back to Africa. The Van Buren administration did not want to run the risk that the court would find the Africans to be free, in which case they could stay in the United States. The administration felt it was better off with the *Amistad* Africans out of the country one way or another.

Five days before the hearing started in Hartford, the Africans were

Spain Upset

As court action proceeded in the *Amistad* case, Spain was losing its patience. In private communications between Spanish officials and the Van Buren administration, they now referred to the Africans as "assassins." Spain was upset because the court case was making it more and more apparent that the Spanish government was allowing the slave trade. That angered Great Britain, the country that had signed a treaty with Spain to end slave trading. Spanish officials were worried Britain would use the treaty violations as an excuse to start a war over Cuba. Spain felt overmatched by Great Britain.

brought onto a canal boat to make the trip from New Haven to the scene of the trial. A huge crowd awaited their arrival. They wondered if the trial would put an end to slavery. ⌒

Secretary of State John Forsyth represented the Van Buren administration during the Amistad trials.

Hartford, Connecticut, in the mid-nineteenth century

OPENING SHOTS

A hush came over the packed courtroom on September 17, 1839, in Hartford, Connecticut, as the trial of the Africans aboard the *Amistad* began. In the mid-nineteenth century, the circuit court handled criminal charges, such as murder and piracy allegations. The district court decided property and salvage issues. In the complicated *Amistad* case, both courts would have to hand down verdicts. The matter was being heard first in the circuit court, which was Judge Smith Thompson's jurisdiction. At the time, this court was located in the state capitol building in Hartford. Judge Judson, who held the hearing onboard the *Washington*, would also hear the case in the district court.

A MATTER OF GOOD VERSUS EVIL

The circuit court opened trial on September 17. The defense attorneys' opening remarks in circuit court took several days to complete. Among other things, the defense painted a dark picture of Montes and Ruiz as evil men who traded in human beings. They wanted to show that Spain was also complicit in that evil by knowingly allowing the slave

Judge Judson

If given the choice, abolitionists likely would not have chosen Judge Judson to hear the *Amistad* case. In 1833, Judson had led a campaign against educating black people. As a member of the Connecticut State Legislature, he helped pass the Black Law, which was aimed at prohibiting black students from coming to Connecticut to attend school. Later that year, as a prosecuting attorney, Judson prosecuted a woman from Canterbury, Connecticut, for the "crime" of attempting to educate black children. However, as public opinion swung in favor of the Africans during the *Amistad* trial, Judson knew he was in a politically difficult position similar to Van Buren's. Ruling either way on the controversial issue could damage his career, so he sought a compromise that would protect him from political harm.

trade to flourish in Cuba. All three defense attorneys—Roger Sherman Baldwin, Seth Staples, and Theodore Sedgwick—addressed the court. The long, gripping opening statements were calculated ploys. The defense attorneys were hoping to monopolize news coverage by controlling the first few days of courtroom activity. They hoped to make the prosecution's case seem unimportant.

The Defense Speaks

The defense started its case by asking for a writ of habeas corpus—a court order freeing a person who has been unlawfully detained. The writ would free the three girls who had been aboard the *Amistad*. After that, the defense attorneys kept the focus squarely on slave trading, slavery, and Spain's role in promoting it.

Baldwin electrified the courtroom. In stark terms, he recounted how the kidnapped

Unforgettable Scene

When the three African girls from the *Amistad* came into the courtroom, they started crying. They tightly grasped the hand of the court matron, who looked after women and children in the jail. As it turned out, they had spotted Ruiz walking into the courtroom. The girls were frightened to see him. Many onlookers saw the youngsters' looks of terror upon seeing Ruiz. The scene was a stinging criticism of slavery.

Capturing a Cuban slave ship, mid-nineteenth century. The defense argued Spain was at fault for allowing the Cuban slave trade.

Africans had fought for their freedom on the *Amistad*. He sketched their current plight: "I say there is no power on earth that has the right again to reduce them to slavery."[1] The defense attorney admonished the court not to make the United States a "slave-catcher for foreign slave-holders."[2] He pointed out that until each one was kidnapped, the Africans had been free individuals. When Lieutenant Gedney arrived on the scene, Baldwin asserted, the Africans were free at that time as well, "not property but human beings."[3]

With a captivated courtroom looking on, Baldwin declared that skin color alone made the difference. He argued:

> It is only when men come here with a black skin that we look upon them in a condition in which they may by any means be made slaves. But when we find them here from the coast of Africa, the same rule must apply to the black as to the white man.[4]

Baldwin proclaimed that, under the laws of the state of Connecticut, people will find that not "every colored man is presumed a slave, until the contrary is shown."[5]

Next, defense attorney Staples told the court that Ruiz was going to take the stand and swear that he did not know the defendants were from Africa. Yet, Staples asserted, Ruiz was well aware that the people

Celebrity Trial

Huge crowds traveled to Hartford for the *Amistad* trial. Reporters from all over the country—and some from foreign countries—descended on the city. Hotel rooms were completely sold out. People packed the streets around the courthouse as well as the courtroom itself. Artists drew pictures of the *Amistad* defendants and sold them outside the courthouse as souvenirs of the event.

he was transporting did not understand Spanish and only spoke a language common to the West African coast. "Let him come here and encounter the perils of perjury, if he dare," Staples bellowed with confidence.[6]

Advocating for Spain

District Attorney William Holabird, representing the US government, restated the Spanish government's strong desire to have the *Amistad*, along with the Africans, returned to Spanish custody. He emphasized how important it was for the US government to uphold its treaties with foreign countries. The only way to settle the case properly, the prosecutor asserted, was to allow President Van Buren to return the Africans to Cuba.

Holabird stated that the prosecution was open to sending the Africans back to their homeland if the court found that they had originally been kidnapped. Lawyers for Ruiz and Montes, as well as Lieutenant Gedney, Captain Green, Captain Ferrer's family, and several Cuban merchants all filed claims with the court. These claims, however, would be settled by the district court in the next phase of the trial.

As the circuit court trial proceeded, the prosecutor presented evidence of the Africans' alleged crimes to a grand jury. A grand jury is a group of citizens who are called upon to determine if there is enough evidence in a case to try the accused in court. The grand jury met in another room in the state capitol building. Montes, Ruiz, and Antonio, the captain's slave, gave testimony to the grand jury.

Arguments went until 7:00 p.m. on Saturday, September 21. The grand jury advised that the circuit court had no jurisdiction to try the Africans for crimes. Judge Thompson would give his decision on Monday, September 23. On Monday, Judge Thompson gaveled the court into session, making it clear that he was against slavery and found it "personally abhorrent." However, he wanted to point out to all those in the courtroom that the decision in this case was not about "the abstract right of holding human beings in bondage."[7]

An Initial Victory

The judge announced his decision. He ruled that the United States had no jurisdiction to try the *Amistad* Africans on murder or piracy charges.

He went on to say that whatever happened aboard the *Amistad* during the revolt happened on a Spanish ship in waters controlled by Spain. The criminal charges against the *Amistad* Africans were dropped. Thompson did not grant a writ of habeas corpus to free the three girls because there were property right claims still pending against the defendants. He said the writ could not be granted until the property issues were settled. Thompson was not going to decide the property claims. Instead, he ruled that the district court should make that decision.

With that, the circuit court concluded its work.

Controversial Arrest

Before the *Amistad* case got under way in district court in November 1839, separate charges were brought against Montes and Ruiz. On behalf of some of the Africans, Tappan pressed charges against Montes and Ruiz, accusing them of assault and battery and false imprisonment. Montes and Ruiz were arrested on October 17, 1839, in New York City, where they were waiting for the *Amistad* trial to start in district court in Hartford. The Spanish government called the arrests scandalous.

The Van Buren administration stepped in. Secretary of State Forsyth said the arrests illegally undermined the powers of the executive branch of government. Forsyth ordered US Attorney Benjamin F. Butler, whose jurisdiction included New York, to get the Spaniards released and to compensate them for wrongful arrest. Both men were given $1,000 bail. Montes left jail and went back to Cuba, never to return to the United States. Ruiz decided to stay in jail as a ploy to gain sympathy for his cause. He received none. Soon, he too posted bail and left for Cuba.

Pricing Human Lives

After Judge Thompson ruled that the *Amistad* Africans could not be tried for murder or piracy, they could have been released on bail. Baldwin requested bail. As the next court action would take place in Judge Judson's court, he decided the bail question. Judson ordered bail equal to what each African would bring on the market if sold as a slave. Repulsed by the idea, the abolitionists refused to post bail. They claimed that, in this case, bail was being used to force them to consider the Africans as slaves with a purchase price.

In the meantime, Judge Judson had opened the district court on September 19, but he quickly decided he needed to know the exact location of the *Amistad* when the *Washington* took it in. He adjourned the court until November 19 in Hartford.

Following the ruling by Judge Thompson on September 23, the Africans were still not free. They returned to jail in New Haven. While waiting for the next court action in November, Cinqué and his companions were being taught English by Yale students. They were also receiving instruction in Christianity.

When the district court came back into session on November 19, 1839, Judge Judson first made a ruling on the issue of jurisdiction. A jurisdiction ruling determines if a matter is being tried in the right court. He found that the *Amistad* was far enough offshore when Gedney took control that the ship was not in New York waters. Therefore, it was in international waters and jurisdiction would depend on where the ship was brought after capture. That happened to be Connecticut.

KEY DEFENSE WITNESSES

One of the key defense witnesses was the interpreter, James Covey. Unfortunately for the defense, Covey was ill and could not travel to Hartford at that time. Another vital defense witness was a British government official, Dr. Richard R. Madden. Madden had served as superintendent of liberated Africans in Cuba. He despised slavery and traveled thousands of miles just to testify in the *Amistad* trial. If the trial proceeded as planned, Covey could not testify. If it was postponed, Madden would have to leave and could not testify.

The defense petition for the trial to be postponed, and Judson agreed to move the trial to January 7, 1840. In the meantime, Judson ruled that Madden should testify by means of a deposition that would be taken immediately. A deposition is sworn testimony taken outside of court. Both the defense and the prosecution could question Madden at the deposition. His written testimony would become evidence when the court hearing resumed in January. Both sides agreed, but the prosecution was not happy when they heard what Madden had to say.

An 1830s drawing of the US slave trade. The district court would decide if the Amistad Africans were free individuals or slaves who could be sold.

Richard Madden testified that Havana, Cuba, was still a major hub of the slave trade.

THE SECOND ROUND

The recorded testimony of Dr. Richard R. Madden in his deposition was eye-opening and highly critical of slavery in Cuba. Madden called Havana, Cuba, the chief commercial center of slave trading. He said slave trading laws were openly violated in Cuba and documents were routinely forged.

District Attorney William Holabird tried to discredit Madden. But with every question Holabird asked, Madden reinforced his testimony and added more detail to the shameful tale of slave trading in Cuba. Following Madden's deposition, the trial was adjourned until January 7, 1840. It seemed like a welcome break for the prosecution. When the trial resumed, it would take place in New Haven, not Hartford. Judson gave no reason for moving the trial. From the standpoint of publicity, however, the Africans had greater support in New Haven than in Hartford.

Preventing Appeal

The break gave both sides time to review their cases. It also gave the administration of President Van Buren time to hatch a new plan to be rid of the *Amistad* case. Secretary of State Forsyth ordered the USS *Grampus* to New Haven harbor. Forsyth was so certain Judson would rule in favor of the administration's position that he wanted everything ready to return the Africans to Cuba immediately. This would prevent the case from being appealed.

Forsyth planned that Cinqué and his companions would be put aboard the *Grampus* right after the decision came down against them and then rushed off to Cuba. Forsyth ordered US marshals in New Haven to whisk the Africans out of the courthouse as soon as the verdict was read. He told the marshals to make sure the *Amistad* Africans were out of New Haven and on the *Grampus* before abolitionists could file an appeal.

Clearly, the Van Buren administration was trying to impose its will on the judicial system by interfering in the appeals process. This raised ethical questions and concerns about abuse of power by the executive branch. The administration was working to circumvent the judicial process.

The Trial Begins

By the time court opened in January, Covey had recovered and was able to testify for the defense.

He testified about what he learned when he first started communicating with the *Amistad* Africans. Covey assured the court that the Africans knew only their native language—no Spanish at all. He said the defendants spoke of beatings and starvation at the hands of the Spaniards. He also told the court his own personal story of having been a slave.

On the second day of the trial, Josiah Gibbs, the language expert from Yale, took the stand. He was testifying about the procedures he used to determine the language Cinqué and his companions spoke. A member of the prosecution began to ask a question when suddenly Judson shocked the courtroom by interrupting. He proclaimed he was "fully convinced that the men were recently from Africa, and it was idle to deny it."[1] This was a ruling in favor of the most important point the abolitionists wanted to make: the Africans were not slaves. Gibbs then quickly completed his testimony. With the question of the Africans' origins settled, the trial continued in order to resolve the property claims.

On the afternoon of the second day of the district court hearing, the courtroom was abuzz. The next witness to be called would be Joseph Cinqué. Finally, the court would hear how one of the captives aboard the *Amistad* had gotten from his homeland to Connecticut—in his own words.

Cinqué Speaks

Courtroom observers were spellbound as Cinqué, speaking through Covey, gave a detailed account of how he was torn from his homeland and forced into slavery. At times, he illustrated his story with actions. He laid down on the courtroom floor to show how he was bound during the long trip from West Africa to Cuba. He startled onlookers as he told of the mistreatment the Africans endured while on the *Amistad*, given only half a cup of water a day.

Artfully Done

Nathaniel Jocelyn, the brother of abolitionist and Amistad Committee member Simeon Jocelyn, was a noted American portrait artist. Originally trained as a watchmaker, he created drawings and oil paintings in his spare time. In 1839, he painted one of the most well-known and enduring portraits of Joseph Cinqué. The portrait was used to help illustrate many stories about the *Amistad* and Cinqué himself.

In an emotional moment, Cinqué concluded his testimony by saying in English, "Give us free."[2] Two other Africans, Grabeau and Fuliwa, got on the stand and confirmed Cinqué's story. As the trial proceeded, the prosecution put witnesses on the stand who only seemed to hurt their case. Antonio,

The Amistad, *eighteenth-century watercolor*

Captain Ferrer's cabin boy, gave a different account of what happened on the *Amistad* than he had before. This made Antonio's testimony seem unreliable. He also stated that the *Amistad* routinely carried slaves from Havana to other parts of Cuba.

Spanish consul Antonio G. Vega was called by the prosecution to discredit the deposition of Dr. Madden. Yet Vega's testimony only confirmed what Madden had said. "There was no law, that was considered in force in the island of Cuba, that prohibited the bringing in [of] African slaves," Vega said under oath.[3] Five days of testimony ended late on a Saturday night. Judge Judson would give his ruling Monday morning.

Silence filled the air as Judge Judson entered the courtroom on Monday morning, January 13. Papers in hand, the judge sat down and began to read. Judson ruled that the Africans were

---

The Remaining Claims

On January 13, 1840, Judge Judson ruled on the other claims in the *Amistad* case as well. He concluded that Lieutenant Gedney and his crew were entitled to a reward—one-third of the value of the ship and its cargo. The Africans unlawfully held captive on the ship would not be considered in assessing the value of that cargo.

Once Gedney received his reward, Spain could have the ship and the cargo back, Judson decided. The Spanish government could then decide who would get the ship and the rest of the cargo on it. In Judson's opinion, Montes, Ruiz, and Spain all failed to prove their cases. He determined that the Africans had been brought into Cuba in violation of Spanish law. Because the slave traders had violated that law, the Africans were free.

Captain Green's claim was denied because Judson determined that he had nothing to do with the seizure of the *Amistad*. Antonio, who was born in Cuba, was a slave and belonged to Captain Ferrer's heirs, the court decreed.

neither slaves nor Spanish subjects. They were free to return to their homeland. The Africans, Judson declared, were born free and ever since had been and still were free. He said the Africans had been kidnapped and sold into slavery in violation of their civil rights. He went on to say that bringing the Africans into Cuba was a violation of Spain's own laws. Because that law was violated, the Africans must go free. As a result, the judge said that no one could claim the Africans as property because they should not have been brought to Cuba in the first place.

THE SECOND VICTORY

Judson's decision was a victory for the abolitionists and the people they were fighting to free. By ruling that the Africans had been kidnapped and must be set free, however, Judson had skirted the property issue. He did not directly address whether the Africans were people or property. He simply decided that the individuals in question were not slaves and were

Nautical Drama

It did not take long for the nation's fascination with the *Amistad* to make it to the stage. By September 2, 1839, just a short time after the rebellion at sea, a play about it opened in New York City. Called *The Black Schooner, or The Pirate Slaver Amistad*, the play opened at the Bowery Theatre and played to full crowds. The playbill called the show a nautical drama featuring piracy, mutiny, and murder. Most of the legal action surrounding the *Amistad* had not yet taken place; therefore, that was not included in the play. Many of the hot-button issues involving slavery were also omitted.

therefore free. He did not make a decision that would end slavery. He managed to keep the case focused on issues specifically involving the *Amistad,* rather than the larger issue of slavery itself.

Stunned by the ruling, Forsyth quietly sent the *Grampus* away from the scene of the trial. He ordered Holabird to appeal the decision to the circuit court. The circuit court, where Judge Thompson presided, heard the appeals. In May 1840, Thompson upheld Judson's ruling. Forsyth told Holabird to appeal the case to the next level—the US Supreme Court, the highest court in the land. ⌐

Joseph Cinqué's moving testimony captivated the courtroom.

The Supreme Court met in the Old Supreme Court Chamber in the US Capitol from 1819 to 1860.

THE FINAL WORD

*I*f a person loses in the Supreme Court, there is no appeal. For the abolitionists, a loss before the highest court in the United States would not only mean a loss of freedom for the *Amistad* Africans. It could mean their deaths if they were turned over to the Spanish, who would likely try them for piracy and murder.

A LEGAL AND POLITICAL HEAVYWEIGHT

For this final legal round, the abolitionists needed all the help they could get. They wanted John Quincy Adams on their team. Once a great orator, Adams was now 73 years old. His hands shook, he was hard of hearing, and his eyesight was failing. He had not tried a case in court in 30 years. Adams himself wondered if he had what it would take to give the Africans the best possible defense. However, he was still one of the greatest legal minds in the nation.

The abolitionists went to meet with Adams in his home in Massachusetts in October 1840. They were unwavering in their belief that Adams, along with Roger Sherman Baldwin, should present the Africans' case before the Supreme Court. Adams had no doubt about the strength of the case. He did, however, doubt his own stamina. To this point, the legal battle had been long and grueling. He wondered if he would be a help or a hindrance to the defense at his age. The cause meant so much to Adams that he rallied himself for one more exhausting legal battle and took the case.

The Supreme Court had nine judges, but five—a majority—were from the South. This meant they were more likely to rule for slavery and against the African defendants. Adams knew that part of his task would be to win over those judges with an eloquent argument for the defense. With the case scheduled to begin in mid-January 1841, Adams was working long hours preparing the case. He would hit hard at the issue of the Van Buren administration's interference in the case. Adams attacked Van Buren so fiercely that the case became known as the trial of one president by another.

In the Supreme Court, unlike in lower courts, witnesses and testimony are not presented. Evidence and testimony given in the lower court is presented to the Supreme Court in the form of written briefs. Lawyers for both sides then deliver oral arguments.

The case was delayed for various reasons and did not get under way in the Supreme Court until February 22, 1841. Even though he was still president, Van Buren had lost most of his power because he lost his reelection bid to William Henry Harrison. Van Buren, a New Yorker, captured Southern votes in the election. But his actions in the *Amistad* case angered Northern voters, and he lost many of his Northern supporters.

Felix Grundy was no longer US attorney general. He ran for a US Senate seat from Tennessee in December 1839 and won. Grundy was succeeded as attorney general by Henry D. Gilpin.

Gilpin presented the government's case before the Supreme Court. Gilpin repeated the Van Buren administration's opinion on the case. He contended that the lower court should have honored Spain's request. He said the *Amistad* and every single thing aboard it, including the Africans, should have been handed over to Spain.

VIOLATIONS OF HUMAN RIGHTS

Roger Sherman Baldwin spoke next. He made a passionate plea for his clients. He charged that Spain was trying to make the United States an accessory to "atrocious violations of

Spanning Three Presidencies

The US Supreme Court started hearing the *Amistad* case in February 1841, when Martin Van Buren was still president. But the court's decision came on March 9, just five days after William Henry Harrison's inaugural address. Harrison died in office on April 4, and Vice President John Tyler took over as the nation's tenth president as the *Amistad* defendants and their supporters were considering how to get them back to Africa.

human rights."[1] He said the Africans aboard the *Amistad* were free people and it was not for the US courts to be "actors in reducing them to slavery."[2] A foreign nation's laws should not be used by the US government to force people into bondage, Baldwin told the justices. He also told the Supreme Court that Ruiz and Montes were guilty of fraud, among other crimes. They had falsified papers to portray the Africans as Cuban natives when they were not.

Following Baldwin's remarks, John Quincy Adams rose to speak. He pointed to a document on the courtroom wall, the Declaration of Independence. He said the guiding principle in the case was at the heart of that document. "I know of no other law that reaches the case of my clients, but the law of Nature and of Nature's God on which our fathers place our national existence," Adams declared.[3] He hammered away at the

Spain Demands Compensation

Even after the US Supreme Court had issued its ruling, Spain tried to get compensation for the *Amistad*, its cargo, and the Africans who were aboard it. Adams fought against this in Congress until his death in 1848. Spain continued to ask every president until Abraham Lincoln for some sort of reparations. Spain finally dropped the matter once and for all at the conclusion of the American Civil War in 1865. Spain's demand for compensation for the *Amistad* was never honored by the United States.

interference of the Van Buren administration in the case, saying that to simply comply with Spanish demands would have been an insult to the US judicial system.

Besides, Adams argued, the Spanish demands were muddled. Did Spain want the Africans returned as property to be given back to their owners or as people to be charged with a crime? In Adams's view, it came down to basic civil rights—the ideals the nation was built on.

On February 25, the case went into recess for several days because Supreme Court Justice Philip Barbour died overnight in his sleep. Now only eight judges would rule on the case. When the case resumed on March 1, Adams completed his remarks. Gilpin then made his rebuttal but offered no new ideas.

Reaching a Decision

The Supreme Court announced that it would hand down a decision on the case on March 9, 1841. Neither side knew what to expect and the atmosphere in the courtroom was heavy with stress and anticipation. Finally, Justice Joseph Story read the court's opinion. The Africans aboard the

Justice Joseph Story read the Amistad *verdict.*

Amistad were not slaves, the Supreme Court ruled
by a 7–1 vote. Therefore, they were free to go. He
emphasized that the Africans had the right to use
self-defense to free themselves from illegal captivity.

The Supreme Court concluded that
the Africans were victims of a heinous
crime because slave trading had been
outlawed. Because they had never
been slaves, Pinckney's Treaty of 1795
did not apply to the *Amistad* Africans.
The prosecution failed to prove that
the Africans were the property of
Montes and Ruiz, Justice Story said.
The court put a dent in the color
barrier by showing blacks had a right
to a fair trial in the US court system.
Only one justice, Henry Baldwin,
had a dissenting opinion.

Eighteen months of legal battles
had come to an end. Cinqué and
his companions were joyful beyond
words. They looked forward to
returning to Africa. Adams wrote
a letter to Lewis Tappan, summing
up his feelings. In the heartfelt note,
the former president said, "Thanks,
in the name of humanity and of
justice . . ."[4]

A Slave No More

The Supreme Court also ruled that Captain Ferrer's cabin boy, Antonio, must be turned over to Ferrer's heirs. That part of the decision almost went unnoticed by the public, but not by the abolitionists. Vehemently opposed to slavery, the abolitionists would not let Antonio be returned to a life of bondage. He simply disappeared. Some claim Antonio went to New York. Others say he was spirited off to Canada. Nothing could be proven. One thing was known for certain: he was never returned to Cuba.

PRELUDE TO FREEDOM

The enormous public interest in the *Amistad* case throughout the United States helped push the divisive issue of slavery to the top of the US agenda. The Africans aboard the *Amistad* told harrowing stories of inhumane treatment, violations of civil rights, and racism. Those who heard these stories knew similar abuses took place in parts of the United States. For many, these abuses were unacceptable in a country founded on principles of individual freedom and human rights.

Getting Home

After the rejoicing over the Supreme Court decision died down, the Amistad Committee still had to find a way to get the Africans home. They asked the current US president, John Tyler, for help, but he offered little assistance. The committee started a fund-raising effort to charter a ship to send Cinqué and his companions home. While they waited, Tappan found lodging for the Africans in Farmington, a small Connecticut town of 2,000 people. Many of the townspeople were members of antislavery societies. The fund-raising effort took on greater urgency when one of the Africans, Foone, was found drowned. Circumstances suggested that he had committed suicide. Delays in returning home might have made him depressed.

Enough funds were finally raised, and in late November 1841, the Africans left on a ship called the *Gentleman*. Five US missionaries went along with the Africans, as did James Covey. After an uneventful voyage, the *Gentleman* arrived in West Africa in late January 1842. Missionaries who accompanied the Africans reported that Cinqué's family had disappeared in a war, but no reliable source records further events in Cinqué's life.

The case tested the moral fiber of the nation. For many, the arguments raised in defense of the *Amistad* Africans challenged slavery itself as an institution utterly contrary to natural law. The Supreme Court ruling in the *Amistad* case did not end the controversy over whether slaves were property. In its decision, the Supreme Court noted that slaves were property, but the Africans aboard the *Amistad* were not proven to be slaves. The abolitionists were not happy with that part of the ruling. While the Supreme Court ruling set the *Amistad* captives free, it did not end slavery in the United States. So the abolitionists continued their fight to end slavery. Though the decision by the Supreme Court was limited in scope, what the public saw and remembered was how slavery was condemned in a legal forum and black people were set free.

The Supreme Court's verdict shook slavery to its core. The historic

A Matter of Civil Rights

Those involved in the *Amistad* case understood the legal wrangling as a battle over the issue of slavery. While the *United States v. the Amistad* definitely focused attention on slavery, few at the time realized that it was also the first civil rights case ever to go before the US Supreme Court. In addition, it turned out to be the first victory in a civil rights case in the Supreme Court. People held against their will, the court ruled, had a right to battle for their freedom. In the area of civil rights, the *United States v. the Amistad* was a precedent-setting case.

ruling made slavery vulnerable to subsequent attack. The decision also energized the abolition movement in the United States and brought it into the mainstream. The courageous and tireless efforts on behalf of the *Amistad* Africans set in motion a long series of assaults on slavery that would eventually result in its end in 1865. ⌐

The Amistad case was a victory for abolitionists in the fight against slavery.

TIMELINE

1839

In January, Joseph Cinqué (Sengbe Pieh) is kidnapped in Mendeland, his homeland in western Africa, and sold into slavery.

1839

In April, Cinqué is put aboard the Portuguese slave ship *Teçora*.

1839

The *Teçora* arrives in Havana in the Spanish colony of Cuba in June.

1839

Between early July and late August, the *Amistad* sails north to the coastal waters of the United States.

1839

The *Amistad* anchors off the Long Island coast on August 25.

1839

Crew members from the USS *Washington* spot the *Amistad*, seize the ship on August 26, and tow it to New London, Connecticut.

1839	1839	1839
Cinqué and 52 other kidnapped Africans are sold to two plantation owners on June 27.	The 53 kidnapped Africans are put on the *Amistad* on June 28 for transport to Puerto Principe.	The kidnapped Africans stage a rebellion aboard the *Amistad* in the early morning of July 2.

1839	1839	1839
Judge Andrew T. Judson holds an investigative hearing on August 29 regarding the *Amistad* Africans.	The Amistad Committee is formed by three abolitionists by September 4.	The US circuit court convenes in Hartford, Connecticut, on September 17 to consider murder and mutiny charges.

TIMELINE

1839

The US district court convenes on September 19 to begin trial for salvage and property claims relating to the *Amistad*.

1839

Judge Smith Thompson rules on September 23 that the *Amistad* Africans cannot be tried for murder or piracy.

1839

Pedro Montes and José Ruiz are arrested in New York City on October 17.

1840

Judge Thompson affirms the district court ruling in May, and the case goes to the US Supreme Court.

1840

In October, John Quincy Adams agrees to represent the *Amistad* Africans before the US Supreme Court.

1841

The *Amistad* case opens in the US Supreme Court in February.

1839

The district court trial opens on November 19 in Hartford before Judge Judson.

1840

The *Amistad* trial in District Court reconvenes on January 7 in New Haven, Connecticut.

1840

Judge Judson rules on January 13 that the *Amistad* Africans are free. The prosecution appeals the decision.

1841

The US Supreme Court rules on March 9 that the *Amistad* Africans are free.

1841

In November, the *Amistad* Africans leave the United States to return to their homeland aboard the *Gentleman*.

1842

The *Gentleman* arrives in Sierra Leone in January. The *Amistad* Africans' long journey is over.

Essential Facts

Date of Event

1839–1841

Place of Event

Mendeland, Africa

Cuba

At sea, the Atlantic Ocean

Long Island, New York

Connecticut

Key Players

John Quincy Adams

Roger Sherman Baldwin

Joseph Cinqué (Sengbe Pieh)

James Covey

William Holabird

District court judge Andrew T. Judson

Pedro Montes

José Ruiz

Lewis Tappan

Circuit court judge Smith Thompson

President Martin Van Buren

Highlights of Event

❖ Joseph Cinqué and 52 other kidnapped Africans were put aboard the *Amistad* in Havana, Cuba, in late June 1839 after being purchased as slaves. Three days after leaving port, the Africans staged a rebellion and seized control of the ship.

❖ After taking control of the *Amistad,* the kidnapped Africans desperately tried to sail home to Africa, but they were captured in the United States in late August 1839.

❖ On September 23, 1839, US circuit court judge Smith Thompson ruled that the *Amistad* captives could not be tried for murder or piracy.

❖ The district court ruled on January 13, 1840, that the *Amistad* Africans were not slaves, they were not subjects of Spain, and they were free to go home. The prosecution appealed the decision all the way to the Supreme Court.

❖ On March 9, 1841, the US Supreme Court ruled in a 7–1 vote that the Africans aboard the *Amistad* were not slaves and were free people.

❖ In November 1841, Joseph Cinqué and his companions began the sea journey home to the west coast of Africa. They arrived in January 1842.

Quote

"It is only when men come here with a black skin that we look upon them in a condition in which they may by any means be made slaves. But when we find them here from the coast of Africa, the same rule must apply to the black as to the white man."
—*Roger Sherman Baldwin*

Glossary

abhorrent
Hateful or despicable.

abolitionist
A person who worked to end the practice of slavery.

assault and battery
A crime involving the threat of violence (assault) and actual violence (battery).

bail
Money paid to allow a prisoner to leave jail temporarily.

complicit
Involved in.

consul
A government official sent to a foreign country to represent the interests of his or her home country.

defendant
A person answering to legal charges in court.

deposition
Testimony taken outside of court to be used in court later.

executive order
A lawfully binding order issued by the president.

grand jury
A jury that decides if the evidence allows formal charges of a crime to be made.

jurisdiction
The right to decide on something in court.

machete
>A large knife used to cut vegetation.

nautical
>Having to do with sailing and the sea.

ploy
>A strategy or tactic.

precedent
>A legal ruling that precedes another and on which a subsequent ruling is based.

prosecution
>The person or group pressing charges against the defendant.

rebuttal
>An argument or proof that refutes or opposes.

salvage
>To reclaim something that was lost.

schooner
>A fast sailing ship.

testimony
>Speech made under oath by a witness in court.

writ of habeas corpus
>A court order issued when a person is unlawfully detained.

ADDITIONAL RESOURCES

SELECTED BIBLIOGRAPHY

Davis, David Brion. *Inhuman Bondage: The Rise and Fall of Slavery in the New World.* New York: Oxford UP, 2008. Print.

Horton, James Oliver, and Lois E. Horton. *Slavery and the Making of America.* New York: Oxford UP, 2006. Print.

Jones, Howard. *Mutiny on the* Amistad: *The Saga of a Slave Revolt and Its Impact on American Abolition, Law, and Diplomacy,* rev. ed. New York: Oxford UP, 1987. Print.

Morgan, Edmund S. *American Slavery, American Freedom.* New York: Norton, 2003. Print.

FURTHER READINGS

Buckley, Susan. *Journeys for Freedom: A New Look at America's Story.* New York: Houghton, 2006. Print.

Grant, Reg. *Slavery.* New York: DK Children, 2009. Print.

Myers, Walter Dean. Amistad: *A Long Road to Freedom.* New York: Puffin, 2001. Print.

Sharp, S. Pearl, and Virginia Schomp. *The Slave Trade and the Middle Passage.* New York: Benchmark, 2006. Print.

WEB LINKS

To learn more about the *Amistad*, visit ABDO Publishing Company online at **www.abdopublishing.com**. Web sites about the *Amistad* are featured on our Book Links page. These links are routinely monitored and updated to provide the most current information available.

PLACES TO VISIT

Amistad Freedom Schooner

Amistad America Inc.
746 Chapel Street Suite 300, New Haven, CT 06510
860-912-9224
amistadamerica.net
A replica of the *Amistad* sails up and down the New England coast and stops at various historic sites throughout the year.

The *Amistad* Memorial

165 Church Street, New Haven, CT 06511
www.edhamiltonworks.com/amistad.htm
This is a monument completed in 1992 to pay tribute to the 53 Africans aboard the *Amistad.* It is on the site of the old New Haven jail, where the Africans were held after their arrest, when the *Amistad* was towed to Connecticut in 1839.

The *Amistad* Research Center

Roger Thayer Stone Center for Latin American Studies at Tulane University
100 Jones Hall, New Orleans, LA 70118
504-865-5164
www.amistadresearchcenter.org
The *Amistad* Research Center has the largest collection of documents in the world dealing with the *Amistad* trials and the events leading up to them. Historians from all over the world visit the center to conduct research on the historic *Amistad* trials.

SOURCE NOTES

Chapter 1. In Freedom's Wake
1. Mary Cable. "Cinqué." *From My People: 400 Years of African American Folklore.* Daryl Cumber Dance, ed. New York: Norton, 2002. Print. 626.

Chapter 2. High Stakes on the High Seas
None.

Chapter 3. Awakening a Nation's Conscience
1. "What the Founders Said about Slavery." *Quotation from Framers of the Constitution . . . and Others.* George Mason University, 2004. Web. 14 Oct. 2010.

Chapter 4. Rallying Support
1. Jeremy Brecher. "The Real *Amistad* Story." *Stone Soup.* Stone Soup, n.d. Web. 14 Oct. 2010.
2. Ibid.

Chapter 5. Strategic Moves
1. "*Amistad:* The Federal Courts and the Challenge to Slavery—Historical Background and Documents." *History of the Federal Judiciary.* Federal Judicial Center, n.d. Web. 14 Oct. 2010.

Chapter 6. Building a Defense

1. Paul Finkelman, ed. "The African Slave Trade and American Courts: The Pamphlets Literature," Series V. *Slavery, Race and the American Legal System 1700–1872*. Clark, NJ: The Lawbook Exchange, Ltd., 2007. Web. *Google Book Search.* 17 Oct. 2010.

2. Ibid.

Chapter 7. Opening Shots

1. Donald Dale Jackson. "Mutiny on the *Amistad.*" *Smithsonian* December 1997: 114–124. Print.

2. Ibid.

3. Howard Jones. *Mutiny on the* Amistad, rev. ed. New York: Oxford U P, 1987. Print. 69.

4. Kareem Abdul-Jabbar and Alan Steinberg. *Black Profiles in Courage: A Legacy of African-American Achievement.* New York: Morrow, 1996. Print. 60.

5. Howard Jones. *Mutiny on the* Amistad. rev. ed. New York: Oxford UP, 1987. Print. 69.

6. Paul Finkelman, ed. "The African Slave Trade and American Courts: The Pamphlets Literature," Series V. In *Slavery, Race and the American Legal System 1700–1872*, 16 vols. Clark, NJ: The Lawbook Exchange, Ltd., 2007. Web. *Google Book Search.* 17 Oct. 2010.

7. Howard Jones. "Impact of the *Amistad* Case on Race and Law in America." *Race on Trial: Law and Justice in American History.* Ed. Annette Gordon-Reed. New York: Oxford UP, 2002. Print. 19.

SOURCE NOTES CONTINUED

Chapter 8. The Second Round

1. Howard Jones. *Mutiny on the* Amistad, rev. ed. New York: Oxford UP, 1987. Print. 122.

2. Arthur Abraham. *The* Amistad *Revolt: An Historical Legacy of Sierra Leone and the United States.* Freetown, Sierra Leone: United States Information Service, 1987; reprinted in 1998 by the United States Information Agency. *Sierra Leone Web.* Sierra Leone Web, 2010. Web. 17 Oct. 2010.

3. Stephen K. Williams, LLD. *Cases Argued and Decided in the Supreme Court of the United States.* Book 10. Rochester, NY: The Lawyers Co-operative Publishing Company, reprint ed., 1911. *Google Book Search.* Web. 17 Oct. 2010.

Chapter 9: The Final Word

1. Roger S. Baldwin. *Argument of Roger S. Baldwin Before the Supreme Court in the Case of US Appellants vs. Cinqué, and Other, Africans of the* Amistad: *1841.* New York: Benedict, 1841. Print. 17.

2. Ibid, 24.

3. Howard Jones. *Mutiny on the* Amistad, rev. ed. New York: Oxford UP, 1987. Print. 176.

4. Ibid, 194.

INDEX

Index Continued

ABOUT THE AUTHOR

Robert Grayson is an award-winning former daily newspaper reporter and the author of books for young adults. Throughout his journalism career, Grayson has written stories on historic events, sports figures, arts & entertainment, business, politics, and pets, which have appeared in national and regional publications, including the *New York Yankees* magazine and *NBA Hoop*.

PHOTO CREDITS

New Haven Colony Historical Society, HO/AP Images, cover, 3, 79, 98 (top); Peeter Viisimaa/iStockphoto, 6; Library of Congress, 9, 27, 33, 51, 55, 61, 73, 90, 95, 96, 98 (bottom), 99; AP Images, 15, 97 (top); Nazia Parvez/AP Images, 16; Steve Dunwell/Photolibrary, 23; Dalin Brinkman/iStockphoto, 24; Hulton Archive/Stringer/Getty Images, 34; Picture History, 41; North Wind Picture Archives/AP Images, 42, 45, 74, 83; Dave Thompson/AP Images, 52; North Wind Picture Archives, 62, 65, 74, 97 (bottom); Bettman/Corbis, 84

DATE DUE